This book is dedicated to the loving memory of my
mentor, colleague, and friend, Jerry Bell.

Contents

Acknowledgments

Throughout my career, I have been blessed to have been able to work with superintendents and other educational leaders in more than 200 public school districts. Without them, this book could not have been written, and for their support I am most grateful. Included in this diverse group of educational leaders are several individuals who have gone beyond the call of duty and to whom I owe a special thank you.

They are: Dick Maxwell, executive director of the Buckeye Association of School Administrators, Columbus, Ohio; Charlie Irish, former superintendent of the Medina City Schools, Medina, Ohio; Harry Eastridge, superintendent of the Educational Service Center of Cuyahoga County, Cleveland, Ohio; Bob Kreiner, superintendent of the Olmsted Falls City Schools, Olmsted Falls, Ohio; Paul Pendleton, former superintendent of schools and current executive director of the Mohican Institute, Columbus, Ohio; Dick Murray, superintendent of the Muskingum Valley Educational Service Center, Zanesville, Ohio; Dave Kircher, former superintendent of the Fairview Park City Schools, Fairview Park, Ohio; Dean Werstler, a former superintendent and current educational consultant who lives in Tucson, Arizona; and Bob McElwee, a human resource development consultant, trainer, and college professor, Orrville, Ohio.

Introduction
Welcome to a New World of Possibility

If you played in your high school's marching band or if you know someone who did, you understand what it is like to spend all day at band camp in the middle of August. The temperature is near 100 degrees and the relative humidity is near 95%, your legs are dead tired, and your brain is on overload trying to learn new music and marching patterns.

Like preparing for a season of marching and playing music, moving to a new level, or new dimension, of thinking is not easy. It takes time and can be hard work. But in the end, the payoff is usually well worth the investment.

Today, there exists a newly discovered world of thought and possibility that is not yet on the radar screen of most people in our society. In this new world, life is more complex yet at the same time simpler than what we have been led to believe. In this new world, many of our most important challenges cannot successfully be met in the same way as they were in the past.

Indeed, like preparing for a season of marching and playing music, entering this new world of possibility can be very challenging. It requires extra effort both intellectually and emotionally—including rejecting old ideas and learning new ones. It requires "thinking outside the box."

In the context of this book, *thinking outside the box* transcends just being creative and coming up with a new angle or technique. It involves a quantum shift in thinking to a different dimension in which we see things in a new light, where unforeseen possibilities appear.

Sometimes these unforeseen possibilities take the form of unwanted, unintended consequences. For example, while eliminating educational programs at first glance may appear to be a good way to balance a school district's budget, doing it may also mask the need for more money, lower the quality of education, and trigger a long-term process of dismantling educational programs.

While thinking outside the box is not always easy, it will strengthen your ability as an educational leader to identify emerging opportunities as well as problems that are hidden from view.

According to Albert Einstein, the significant problems we face cannot be solved at the same level of thinking we used when we created them. New possibilities require fresh, open, and unrestricted vision.

The chapters that follow are synergistic. Like the pieces of a mosaic, they are interconnected and work together to form a reservoir of thought that will enable you to sharpen the focus of the lens through which you view the world.

With this new focus, you will improve your ability to safely navigate the rough waters of change that are surging across the educational landscape today.

* * *

Although *Thinking Outside the Box* can be read in an afternoon, it is not about silver bullets and other quick fixes. Rather, it is a personal invitation to begin a journey into a new world of thought and possibility.

Throughout the book, references are made to visionaries who live on the leading edge of this new world. Hopefully, this book will inspire you to continue your journey by reading their works.

CHAPTER 1

Take to Heart the Words of Edmund Burke

When my brother and I were little, we used to wake up on Saturday morning and spend three or four hours glued to our television sets watching "Bugs Bunny," "Mighty Mouse," and other popular cartoons. Sometimes, we'd even be allowed to have one or two of our friends over.

Although it has been a long time since Mike and I sat around in our pajamas watching cartoons, I vividly recall one episode of the popular cartoon "Tweety Bird and Sylvester." In it, Sylvester has Tweety Bird trapped in his paws and is about to eat him when an angel-like replica of Sylvester suddenly appears on his shoulder and begs him not to eat the bird. As Sylvester weakens and begins to reconsider whether or not to eat Tweety Bird, a devil-like replica of Sylvester appears on the cat's other shoulder and implores him not to be a wimp and to go ahead and eat the bird.

This episode of "Tweety Bird and Sylvester" portrays what is occurring today in many parts of our society where an age-old battle between two legendary forces continues to take place. Like Sylvester's heart and mind, our newly discovered world of power and possibility continues to serve as a battleground for the age-old forces of good and evil (i.e., positive and negative thinking).

Today, the amount of conflict and turmoil taking place in our schools, churches, businesses, and other public and private institutions is growing at an alarming rate. And it is not all happening by accident. Driven by a large reservoir of pent-up frustration, disappointment, and anger, some people are so upset that they have become experts at stirring the pot and coalescing the negative thinking of others.

Knowing that there is a constant battle, or tension, occurring between positive and negative forces in our schools and communities, what do you as an educational leader do about it?

The answer is simple: You wake up the choir of good-hearted people in your schools and communities who aren't trapped by their negative feelings and who want to do what is best for children.

However, doing this is not quite as simple as it may sound, because our culture has taught us that we shouldn't waste our time preaching to the choir. As a result, we either ignore the choir or put it to sleep with good news, which in turn makes us increasingly vulnerable to the forces of negative thinking.

So, rather than put the choir to sleep, we need to awaken it. We need to take to heart the words of British statesman and parliamentary orator Edmund Burke, who played a prominent role in political issues from 1765 to 1795: "The only thing necessary for evil to triumph is for good men to do nothing."

Key Thought

Empower good-hearted people to go out
and make a difference.

CHAPTER 2

Escape the Cult of Efficiency

Generally speaking, educational leaders have a love-hate relationship with business. While they hate the negative way in which they feel many business leaders in our country have portrayed them, they love to model business practices in their schools.

Take, for example, the widely accepted idea that the public schools should function like a business and be lean and accountable. In their zeal to be good stewards of the tax dollar, many educational leaders unintentionally dismantle important educational programs and lower academic standards. To be efficient like their business counterparts, they cut their budget—and with it, valuable services that their students need.

As one educational leader put it, "Schools don't run out of money. They run out of education. As long as we keep making cuts, it is relatively easy to stay in the black."

Some educational leaders, for example, have bought into the suggestion from the business sector that to be more efficient they should privatize school services such as food service and transportation. Of course, this is easier said than done and when not done correctly can generate negative unintended consequences.

While privatizing school district services such as transportation and food service may seem more efficient, it may also cost you more money than it saves. Unless your employees are comfortable with the idea of bringing in an outside concern to run their operation, the negative side effects can be costly.

The Hidden Costs of Privatizing Services

1. Upset classified employees can easily infect the attitude of the teaching staff.
2. Together, the classified employees and teachers begin to view other issues in a negative light and vent their anger and frustration to the community.
3. When it comes time to negotiate new contracts, school employees are not in a good mood and the price to appease them escalates.
4. At tax levy time, the employees are reluctant to listen to why the money is needed—let alone work in the campaign.
5. If the employees do not want privatization to work, they can drive up the costs and sabotage it.
6. Eventually, those disenchanted members of the community who are always looking for ways to bash the schools suddenly sense what is going on, and they have a field day with this negative information.
7. Finally, when the schools need to pass a tax levy or make some other important decision, the seeds of negativity that have been planted among the school employees as well as the community undercut the support needed to implement the decision.

This is a classic example of where the cure (privatization) is worse than the disease (inefficiency). In fact, in this instance, the cure actually increases inefficiency.

The "cult of efficiency" has deep historical roots. Comprehensively chronicled in Raymond Callahan's seminal book, *Education and the Cult of Efficiency: A Study of the Social Forces That Have Shaped the Administration of the Public Schools* (1962), the cult of efficiency has a stranglehold over the mindset of the culture in which educational leaders live and work.

Being efficient for its own sake (i.e., "the cult of efficiency") can generate a wide range of negative, unintended consequences. As an educational leader, it is important that you escape the cult of efficiency.

Key Thought

Saving money in the short run
may cost you more money in the long run.

CHAPTER 3

Beware of Ducks and Politics

"If it looks like a duck and acts like a duck, then it must be a duck."
This commonly used phrase serves as a good segue to the following
story about something that occurs all too often in school districts across
our nation.

School officials and campaigns workers were worn out as they pre-
pared to organize the third campaign in a single year to pass a much-
needed school tax issue. The first two attempts failed by wide margins.

Angry, frustrated, and desperate, they contacted a local political consultant to see if he could provide some answers.

A hard-nosed veteran of years of inner-city political wars, the consultant offered two tantalizing ingredients necessary to a successful
campaign. First, he was an expert at manipulating voters and knew how
to get the Yes voters to the polls. Second, he said he would handle the
entire campaign with his crew of mass-media advertising experts.

The potential for a painless and effortless quick fix was so inviting
that the citizens' committee hired his firm to do whatever it would take
to pass the tax issue. And that is exactly what the political consulting
firm did.

With the worn-out school officials and campaign workers sitting in
the stands, the firm executed a slick and well-conceived media blitz
that resulted in a narrow margin of victory on election day. The campaign strategy was to identify school supporters and use threats of losing bus service and athletic programs to get them to the polls.

As a short-term fix, the strategy worked. However, in addition to creating an election victory, this strategy of manipulation generated distrust
and resentment—even among those who voted for the tax proposal.

While they went along with the idea of leveraging *yes* votes to avoid the possibility of cutting busing and athletics, many school supporters knew that these were trumped-up threats, and that the amount of money to be saved by the cuts in these areas would be minimal.

What was not discussed, nor apparent, was that the real educational crisis that underpinned the need to pass a tax issue never surfaced. The true reason for urgency wasn't the possible loss of bus service or athletics. It was the loss of teachers and educational programs. School officials had made nearly all of the nonclassroom cuts that were available to them and, because of the size of the budget deficit facing the district, the next step would have been the elimination of teachers and important educational programs.

Unfortunately, this was not common knowledge. Instead of focusing on the true reason for urgency that existed, the message being carried on the community grapevine was how school officials had outsmarted the voters with a brilliantly conceived political strategy and passed their levy.

In the process of winning the battle, however, the school board had taken a giant step toward losing the war. While it had won a short-term victory at the polls, by waging a campaign strategy of deceit and duplicity, it also had planted large seeds of distrust and resentment among school employees and community members.

As a result, rather than coming across as community leaders and statesmen, the board had relegated itself to the role of politicians.

So, getting back to the duck analogy, if these educational leaders looked like politicians and acted like politicians, then they must have been politicians. And in this day and age, that is not perceived as a good thing.

For many reasons, our citizenry is growing more and more disenchanted with our nation's large institutions, and our political system ranks at the top of the list of institutions people are disenchanted with—or perhaps it is the bottom of the heap.

However, just as the educational culture adopted the cult of efficiency to organize schooling at the turn of the last century, it also co-opted many of the communication strategies of the late twentieth-century political arena. One of these strategies is the practice of spinning messages to accentuate the positive and downplay the negative.

When I meet with educational leaders in workshops and seminars and we focus on this habit of spinning messages to put the schools in the best possible light, I don't mince words. I call it what it is: manipulation.

Interestingly, when I do this, I receive recognition responses from nearly everyone in the room. They know it is manipulation and, more importantly, so does everyone else. In this day and age, the public has been educated to know when it is being manipulated by our political leaders—which is why trust in our political system is gradually withering away.

Today, there is a desperate need at all levels of our society for what is called *authentic leadership*. In *The Human Side of School Change: Reform, Resistance, and the Real-life Problems of Innovation* (1996), Robert Evans says that authentic leaders are distinguished not by their techniques or styles but by their integrity and their savvy. And by savvy he means practical competence—including craft knowledge, life experience, native intelligence, common sense, intuition, courage, and the capacity to handle situations.

So, if you are a school administrator and want to look like a trusted leader rather than a duck or a politician, then act with integrity. Rather than spinning what you or your district says in order to look good, square with people. Not only can they handle being leveled with, they are desperately seeking it today and will respond in the most positive of ways.

Key Thought

Telling the whole truth builds trust
and fosters understanding.

CHAPTER 4

Don't Accept Other People's Monkeys

Imagine for a minute that a corporate manager is walking down the hall and notices one of his subordinates, Mr. A, coming up the hallway. When they are abreast of one another, Mr. A greets the manager with, "Good morning. By the way, we've got a problem. You see. . . ." The manager says, "So glad you brought this up. I'm in a rush right now. Meanwhile, let me think about it and I'll let you know." Then he and Mr. A part company.

Now, let's analyze what has just happened. Before the two of them met, on whose back was the "monkey"? The subordinate's. After they parted, on whose back was it? The manager's. Subordinate-imposed time begins the moment a monkey successfully executes a leap from the back of a subordinate to the back of his superior and does not end until the monkey is returned to its proper owner for care and feeding.

"Management Time: Who's Got the Monkey?" is the title of a groundbreaking article published in the *Harvard Business Review* in 1974. Written by two management consultants, the article addresses the question of why managers are typically running out of time while their subordinates are typically running out of work. The authors conclude that most managers spend much more subordinate-imposed time than they even faintly realize.

In public school administration, time is a scarce commodity, and what there is of it is divided among a growing list of administrative demands. To complicate matters, the culture in which educational leaders operate provides little or no management training, discourages delegation, and encourages accepting other people's monkeys.

In addition to the proverbial vow of poverty that educators take when they join the educational profession, educational leaders are taught to say, "Yes, we'll make do but we'll also make it work" and "No, we don't need to spend money on badly needed administrative support because we understand that the public doesn't want to waste money on administration."

So, what happens? Most educational leaders wear themselves out doing things that others should be doing and then have little time to provide the educational leadership that is needed today.

It's like the fellow who gets himself in a traffic jam, takes the off ramp and starts flying through the back country. Although he doesn't have a clue where he's going, he is happy as a clam because he's making good time.

What then are some of the monkeys that educational leaders need to get off their backs? Here is a partial list of items—some of which are tongue-in-cheek but also are essentially true:

"As an educational leader. . . ."
I should smile and say Yes whenever I am asked to do something because making people happy is my job.
I am personally responsible for passing school tax issues.
I must attend every school event.
I should spend the lion's share of my time completing administrative forms.
I need to do the work my secretary can't get done because she is administering medication and doing other chores that someone else could be doing.

Well, I could list additional examples of how educational leaders accept other people's monkeys, but you probably get my point that carrying around monkeys is hard work. Sometimes they are so heavy that they become a great burden both physically and psychologically. They also can serve as an impediment to effective decision making because those who need to be shouldering the responsibility are excluded from doing so.

Key Thought

When you do things others should be doing,
it wastes your time, limits what you
are able to accomplish, and sets you up
as a scapegoat for the mistakes of others.

CHAPTER 5

Eliminate Nagging Problems

Little things don't just mean a lot. They can mean everything.

Oftentimes, we don't get into trouble over big problems because big problems are easy to identify and, as a result, tend to get resolved. Rather, it is the little nagging problem that, if left alone too long, can do the real damage.

Nagging problems are usually difficult to clearly define and involve personal relationships. So rather than confront the situation, the problem is allowed to continue and, if allowed to fester over time, can become an albatross for an educational leader and even lead to his or her downfall.

A few years ago, an outstanding educational leader in a small rural school district in the Midwest saw his credibility and effectiveness seriously undercut by a nagging problem. The culprit was a school employee and long-time resident of the school district. While less than competent, the employee didn't seem to be doing that much damage. So the easy decision was to make no decision and just let him continue doing his thing.

However, it wasn't quite that simple. As a highly visible member of the school district's administrative team, he was under the microscope of both the school district's employees and the general public. So every time he made a bad decision or tripped up in some other manner, it became common knowledge throughout the school district.

As the situation continued, many residents began questioning why this person was allowed to remain in his job. Some even started pointing fingers at his boss, the superintendent of schools, who they felt was allowing the situation to go on unabated.

Eventually, the superintendent became a target of widespread criticism and ultimately was fired. Ironically, however, his nagging problem remained on the job.

Another example of how a nagging problem can lead to big trouble involved an elementary school in a fast-growing, upscale suburban district in the Northeast. In this particular school, a number of significant changes had been handed down from the top administration and, predictably, some of the teachers were not excited about the situation.

One of the disenchanted teachers was a veteran who possessed extraordinary power and influence over the rest of the elementary staff. She was highly skilled in stirring the pot and making life miserable for the principal of her building. In fact, she intimidated both her peers and her principal.

Rather than confront this veteran teacher, her building principal ignored the situation and hoped that it would go away. But it didn't. In fact, it grew worse and eventually forced the district superintendent to assign a new principal to the building.

And, yes, you guessed it. The cycle started over again with the new building principal.

These two examples of nagging problems are not isolated instances. These kinds of situations are occurring in schools across America every day and they cannot be ignored.

Key Thought

When you allow nagging problems to fester,
they infect your entire organization and
ultimately your credibility.

CHAPTER 6

Lead from Your Heart

I remember it as if it were yesterday. We had just ended a light work-out under the lights in preparation for our third high school football game of the year. Following a loss and a tie, it was our moment of truth and we knew it.

One more defeat and we not only would kiss our hopes for another league championship good-bye, but we'd end three straight years of near-perfect seasons. At the end of practice, we decided to meet without our coaches at the far west end of our stadium and address our fate.

As we talked among ourselves, the words of encouragement that our coaches had been giving us since junior high school echoed in our heads. And their message was this: Whoever truly believes in themselves and has the most heart usually wins.

Well, the rest is history. Inspired by our strong desire and will—we called it Bulldog pride back then—to continue our winning tradition, we won our remaining games and captured our fourth straight South-western Buckeye League title.

Even though it happened nearly 40 years ago, I've never forgotten this experience because it wasn't just about winning football games. As I fondly reflect upon that life-changing experience, it becomes clearer each passing day that what we were able to accomplish on the football field four decades ago was not the result of just good timing or luck. It was about something else.

While we weren't blessed with an abundant amount of athletic talent, our will to win was stronger than anyone else in our conference. We knew in our hearts that we could triumph and we somehow turned that heartfelt confidence into positive action on the football field.

In *Leading with Soul* (1995), Lee Bolman and Terry Deal focus on the power of leading from the heart and how it can make a difference both for ourselves and for others. They believe that the heart of leadership lies within the hearts of leaders.

The two authors explain that in recent years we have fooled ourselves into thinking that sheer bravado or sophisticated techniques could respond to our deepest concerns. They contend that as a society we have lost touch with a most precious human gift—our spirit.

To recapture that spirit, they say we need to relearn how to lead with soul. We need to breathe new zest and buoyancy into life and reinfuse both the family and the workplace with passion and purpose.

In her book, *The Healing of America* (1997), Marianne Williamson also focuses on the power of leading from the heart. She explains that where people are separate from each other—when they are angry, polarized, and defensive—breakdown and disorder are inevitable. She believes that we must reclaim our capacity to think and feel as powerfully and deeply as possible, and expand our capacity to love.

Keeping all of this in mind, let's look at what can happen when a principal meets with his or her teachers and introduces a new state-mandated educational strategy for their building. While some of the teachers get excited about the chance to try new ideas, others take it as a criticism of their existing teaching competencies and grow anxious about the changes they may have to make in what they teach and how they teach it. Although the reasons for the mandated changes may make logical sense for the staff members, their hearts are heavy with a mixture of anger, fear, and disappointment.

However, what if the principal first sits down with his or her teachers, explains with deep compassion and understanding of their concerns about the educational changes being mandated, and then gives them time to figure out how they can take advantage of the changes that are about to occur? Yes, leading from the emotion of the heart rather than the logic of the head says to the teachers that they matter, possess great value, and can make a difference.

Thus, at the core, the power of leadership is in our hearts, not our heads. Since our emotional connection with others is much stronger than is our intellectual connection, how we feel about what we say is far more important than what we say. Our passion and integrity are what inspire others to follow our words and join us in our journey to make a difference.

As an educational leader, leading from your heart can serve as an emotional magnet to turn chaos into consensus.

Key Thought

Inspiring others with your heartfelt passion
triggers a domino effect that works
through your entire organization.

CHAPTER 7

Embrace Controversy

Another belief deeply embedded in our educational culture is that educators should avoid controversial issues that divide their schools and community. Controversy and conflict, however, are usually symptoms of deeper problems that, if not identified and defused, will fester and contaminate everything they touch. And the longer conflict and controversy are avoided, the more angry and frustrated people become that their issues and concerns are being ignored.

In addressing controversial issues in a school district, the underlying message to school employees and community residents is that "you count and your feelings are important." Even when school officials are not in a position to give people what they want, just addressing their concerns in a genuine and caring manner creates huge deposits of good will and support.

A good example of turning controversy into good will and support occurred in Medina, Ohio, when the American Civil Liberties Union (ACLU) challenged the right of the local school officials to have a picture of Jesus hanging in one of their elementary buildings. Some residents said, "Fight it. Don't let the ACLU push you around." Prayer meetings were held throughout the community and the superintendent received letters and calls from across the country urging him and his board of education to "keep Jesus in school." Others, however, were equally vocal—imploring the school board to remove the picture.

Against the advice of many people on both sides of the issue, the superintendent and board of education decided not to act until they heard from the community. And that is what they did.

As you can imagine, the boardroom was packed to the gills with residents representing both sides of this controversial and emotional issue. The tension was so thick that you could cut it with a knife. For the first hour, a parade of citizens vented their emotions, which included charges and countercharges. Since there was no one else to whom to vent, most of the anger and frustration was directed toward the school board. However, the board members didn't argue. Instead, they just listened until a solution emerged, and the picture ultimately found a new home in the chapel of a church located across the street from the elementary school.

A community survey conducted a few weeks later found that, while the school district's handling of the situation had not changed many people's minds about the picture, it had increased community trust in the school system because of the sensitivity exhibited by school officials. However, if school officials in Medina had believed that they should have avoided the controversy about having a picture of Jesus in one of their school buildings, they would have sent the wrong message to the residents of their community and made a bad situation even worse.

The next chapter continues the discussion of the inherent power of validating the feelings of others.

Key Thought

*Embracing controversy can defuse problems
and generate the will and wherewithal
to solve them.*

CHAPTER 8

Validate the Feelings of Others

If you've ever been a high school principal, you've probably had to deal with this kind of situation—and probably on more than one occasion.

It is springtime and graduation ceremonies are rapidly approaching. In the lead for valedictorian are two students, both of whom have had straight As throughout their high school career.

The only thing that separates them are their grades for the final nine-week recording period. When the grades are reported, one of the students receives all As while the other receives a B in physical education and the rest As.

As it turns out, the student had received the B because he had skipped two P.E. classes while pursuing an academic scholarship at a widely respected university. When his parents learned of the B and the lost opportunity to be his high school's valedictorian, they became enraged.

Predictably, they stormed into the high school principal's office and demanded to know why their son had received the B and what could be done about it. Rather than overreacting to their anger, the principal sat quietly and listened intently to their pleas for help.

When the parents completed their 15-minute outpouring of frustration and disappointment about their son's predicament, the principal responded with deep empathy and a clear understanding of their situation. By responding in this way, he defused much of the negative emotion of the parents.

The principal explained that the school district had spent two years developing a way to deal with these kinds of situations and then asked the parents what they would do if they were sitting in the principal's chair. Yes, as you might expect, with the anger diluted, if not out of the way entirely, the parents said they would do exactly as the principal had done and award valedictorian honors to the other student. In fact, they agreed that the lesson to be learned by their son will be much more valuable than their pulling strings to break the rules for him.

By genuinely empathizing with the plight of parents, the principal met what Stephen Covey contends is our primary psychological need. In *The Seven Habits of Highly Effective People* (1989), Covey explains that a person's greatest psychological need in life is not to be agreed with but to be validated—which enables them to feel they have value as a human being. So, one of the most powerful thing you can do as an educational leader is, in Covey's words, "seek first to understand and then to be understood."

Seeking first to understand means truly understanding the point of view of another person or group of persons. Empathic listening is deeply therapeutic because it gives people psychological "air." Once they sense they are understood, they lower their defenses.

The trick is to make the distinction between the terms *validation* and *agreement*. When we validate the feelings of another person, we don't necessarily have to agree with their point of view. We simply need to let them know through our body language that how they feel is important and valid.

When we realize that we don't have to agree with others in order to validate them, it is a lot easier to defuse potential conflict and work through strong feelings.

Another good example of how validation can heal old wounds occurred a few years ago in a small Ohio school district near Cleveland. Following the defeat of two school bond issues, the board of education conducted a community opinion survey to find out why residents had voted "No" and by sizable margins.

The results of the survey were eye-opening. Without prompting, half of the residents said that they were angry because the previous school board had ignored the advice of a blue-ribbon committee it had created to assess the condition of the district's school buildings.

Whether or not the advice was really ignored didn't matter. At this point, it had become the public perception of residents in the school district. And by ignoring the advice of the committee members who had taken time from their busy schedules to study the situation and make a recommendation, the school board said, in essence, that "your opinions aren't worth the paper on which they are written."

The situation had turned into a breach of faith for many residents who knew the school board members personally and had trusted them. The disappointment and anger was deeply felt and widespread.

To ease the emotional pain that many residents still felt, the new school board, which had conducted the community survey, drafted a letter and mailed it to every residence in the district. The letter, which appears below and was signed by each of the five school board members, triggered a dramatic turnaround that not only restored the trust that had been lost but also served as the catalyst for ultimately passing the bond issue:

Dear School District Residents,

Thank you for taking time to participate in the recent community survey. The response was excellent. More than 1,000 households completed the survey questionnaire.

While we are pleased that the majority of residents have a positive attitude toward their school system and feel it is providing a quality education, it is very clear from the survey responses that one particular issue is a major source of anger, concern, and disappointment in this school district. Nearly half of the residents responding think "the Middle School" should have been built first.

It is clear from the results of this survey that many residents did not agree with the sequence of building projects. Therefore, they perceived the decision to be a violation of the trust and confidence they place in their local school board.

At this point in time, however, we cannot change past events—nor do we intend to second-guess the members of the school board who made the difficult decision in 1990 to address the overcrowding conditions in the elementary buildings before focusing on the middle school problem. What we can do, as the current school board members, is accept full responsibility for what has happened, to respond to the public concern that currently exists, and to pledge to continue to improve our communication with the community.

We understand how many of you feel, since three of us served on the Facilities Planning Committee in 1989. For those of you who are still disappointed or upset by the situation, please accept our sincere apology.

Following the mailing, members of the school board received many positive phone calls from residents who said they appreciated the fact that someone finally took the time to listen to them and to really understand how they felt.

Key Thought

Most people need to be understood
more than they need to be right.

CHAPTER 9

Do What All Great Managers Do

True or false?

The lower the millage (taxes), the easier it is to pass school tax issues.

Most residents have a good idea of what school is like today.

Delegating responsibility to citizen task forces creates community ownership.

Athletics are a high priority for the majority of residents.

The public is not happy with the quality of education being provided in their school system.

Parents with children in school are much more supportive of their schools than are other school district residents.

With enough information, most people will see the light.

Publicizing school improvement programs builds trust and credibility.

The public schools should be run like businesses.

The correct answer for all of this conventional wisdom is: false.

When framed in the context of our new world of possibility, conventional wisdom not only fails to deliver on its promises, but it also takes educational leaders down the primrose path of unintended consequences.

Take, for example, the conventional wisdom that says the lower the millage, the easier it is to pass school tax issues. In reality, unless the millage being requested is very low or very high, it is a relatively minor factor in determining the outcome of a school tax election and the reason is this: Millage is a No-voter issue, not a Yes-voter concern, and No voters nearly always vote No, no matter how high or low the millage is.

Yes voters are motivated by educational need. The greater the need, the more likely it is that they will be motivated enough to get out and vote.

However, as a result of the conventional thinking of their profession, most educational leaders try to keep the millage as low as possible with the hope that it will help assure passage of their tax issue. Sometimes, after losing an election, they panic and even reduce the millage for the next election in hopes that the voters will be appreciative and vote Yes.

School officials also make commitments to their residents to keep tax issues off the ballot for as long as possible—often shackling themselves to a specific number of years—in order to demonstrate fiscal accountability and generate good will. Unfortunately, these strategies usually backfire. Instead of motivating Yes voters to get out and vote, they reinforce the feeling among No voters that the schools are wasting money and can afford to reduce expenses. And rather than keeping the millage down, the need for more money (and the millage level) increases the longer a school board waits to place a tax issue on the ballot.

In an in-depth study of 80,000 managers, the largest of its kind ever undertaken, The Gallup Organization discovered the one thing that great managers do across the board, despite their individual differences. While they differ in sex, age, and race, employ vastly different management styles, and focus on different goals, great managers do not hesitate to break virtually every rule held sacred by conventional wisdom.

Gallup found that these great managers aren't limited to a particular profession or occupation. They are hotel supervisors, manufacturing team leaders, sales managers, senior account executives, professional sports coaches, religious leaders, pub managers, military officers, and public school superintendents.

As Marcus Buckingham and Curt Coffman state in *First, Break All the Rules* (1999), a book which grew out of the Gallup study, "conventional wisdom" is conventional for a reason: It is comfortingly and seductively easier. It is easier, for example, to accept rather than to challenge the belief that the public schools should be run like businesses.

The wisdom of great managers, however, is not easy. It is much more exacting and demands discipline, focus, trust, and the willingness to individualize.

Great managers look for the exceptions rather than the rules of conventional wisdom to frame their beliefs and guide their actions.

Key Thought

Challenge the conventional wisdom
that drives what others in your profession do.

CHAPTER 10

Don't Try to Change Old Dogs or People

The following is a familiar story. It is familiar because many educational leaders continue to buy into the security and teaching-by-the-numbers feel it provides.

Triggered by the publication of "A Nation at Risk" in 1983, the school reform bandwagon was off and running. With the introduction of effective teaching practices springing forth like a field of dandelions after a good rain, educational leaders began to prescribe not only what should be taught but how it should be taught.

One of the most popular pioneers in the educational reform movement was Madeline Hunter, who in the early 1960s identified what she considered to be the seven most basic components of an effective lesson plan. Thousands of school administrators soon became her disciples and not only trained their teachers in the seven steps but also evaluated each teacher based upon how closely and how well they followed the required sequence. What began as a thoughtful message to help teachers to improve their teaching became a creed that many teachers were forced to recite.

Today, however, a growing number of educational leaders understand that the essence of great teaching is to treat every child as an individual, and that can't be done by following seven steps. They are finding, as did the great managers in the Gallup study, that any attempt to impose a "one best way" is doomed to fail.

When people are forced to do things in a narrowly prescribed way, they become both resentful and dependent. Forcing them into the same "one best way" box prevents them from utilizing the unique talents they developed in their teenage years. It prevents them from doing it "*their* best way."

This story is not an indictment of Madeline Hunter. Rather, it is a word of caution for those who believe we can train people to do not only what we want them to do but how we want them to do it.

During the past decade, neuroscience has discovered that by the time we reach our early teens, our brain has carved out a unique network of synaptic connections. These mental pathways become our filter, producing the recurring patterns of behavior that make us unique.

This does not mean that we can't change. We can learn new knowledge and new skills, alter our values, and develop a greater sense of self-awareness. However, beyond our mid-teens there is a limit to how much our character can be recarved.

In its study of 80,000 managers in over 400 companies, Gallup discovered that the world's greatest managers believe that people don't change that much. The study uncovered the fact that great managers believe we are wired to think and behave in certain ways and that it is a waste of time trying to put in what was left out.

Instead, try to draw out what was left in. Identify recurring patterns of thought, feeling, and behavior and match them with roles that are a good fit. Some of us, for example, have a natural ability or talent to remember names, while others remember faces. Some of us have a talent for being nurturing and caring, while others possess the natural ability to cut to the quick and make things happen.

If you are an elementary principal, being nurturing and caring is a valuable and important talent—and not just because you are working with young children. Most elementary teachers also thrive when they are working in a nurturing environment.

So, whoever first coined the expression that "you can't teach an old dog new tricks" is right on target. If you don't train him while he is a puppy, his natural predisposition to do things "his best way" rather than a "one best way" will limit what you can teach him after his mid-teens (in dog years, of course).

Key Thought

Help people use their natural talents
to help you succeed.

CHAPTER 11

Get the Right People on the Bus

It is nearly impossible to get rid of a tenured teacher.

It is safer to ride it out with a weak employee than to risk a lawsuit and the negative publicity that goes with it.

It is a hassle to document the evidence required to fire someone.

It is easier to move a person who is in the wrong spot to a position where they will do less damage.

It is growing more and more difficult to find good people today.

It is impossible to keep good people because we're unable to compete with what other school districts are able to offer.

These are just some of the reasons why educational leaders fail to get the right people on the bus and get the wrong people off the bus. In this instance, the bus riders include everyone—school board members, administrators, teachers, and nonteaching staff.

However, in the current era of continuous improvement and with the goal of no child left behind, the need for educational leaders to get the right people on the bus and the wrong people off the bus has never been greater. This point is reinforced by the results of a national study conducted by Jim Collins, a former faculty member at the Stanford University Graduate School of Business who now works from his management research laboratory in Boulder, Colorado.

In 1996, Collins undertook a five-year research project to identify U.S. companies that have made the leap from generating good to great financial results and have then sustained these great results for at least 15 years. Eleven companies emerged from the pack as making the grade.

In analyzing why these companies were able to go from good to great and sustain it, he found that a few key factors made most of the difference. One of those factors is making sure you have the right people on the bus.

In his book, *Good to Great: Why Some Companies Make the Leap . . . and Others Don't* (2001), Collins writes that good to great leaders understand three simple truths about the importance of getting the right people on the bus. First, if you get the right people on the bus, you can more easily adapt to a changing world. If they are on the bus because of who else is on the bus rather than where the bus is headed, it is much easier to change direction when needed.

Second, if you have the right people on the bus, the problem of how to motivate and manage people largely goes away. The right people don't need to be tightly managed and fired up. They will be self-motivated by the inner drive to produce results and their desire to be a part of something great.

Third, if you have the wrong people on the bus, it doesn't matter whether you discover the right direction for the bus ride. Great vision without great people is irrelevant.

Unfortunately, instead of getting the right people on the bus and the wrong people off the bus, many educational leaders follow the conventional wisdom of trying to "fix those who need fixing" that are currently on the bus. They conduct personality inventory tests, bringing in team building consultants and other trainers in an attempt to make do and not rock the boat.

However, as you read in the previous chapter, people are who they are from an early age and they don't change in any fundamental way. As a result, more emphasis needs to be given to getting the right people on the bus and the wrong people off it, and less emphasis given to trying to change those who are already there.

Key Thought

*Hire people who are motivated by an inner drive
to produce results and be a part of something great,
and get rid of those who aren't.*

CHAPTER 12

Confront the Brutal Facts

For as long as most people can remember, the Hometown Schools enjoyed the reputation of being one of the best school districts in the state. Each year, the school system generated several National Merit Scholars and that, along with other indicators of success, helped perpetuate the district's high quality image.

However, the demographic makeup of the school district was changing. While National Merit Scholars continued to live in the district, inner-city families and others who were attracted to the fine reputation of both the community and the school system were migrating there.

The brutal facts were clear: Hometown was changing and that change was being reflected in the makeup of the student body of its school system.

Fortunately, Hometown's educational and community leaders didn't succumb to the temptation of sticking their heads in the sand and denying that these demographic changes were taking place. Instead of living in the past and doubling their effort to preserve the old reality of educational excellence, they confronted situations head-on and began to create a working model of excellence based upon the current reality.

What caused the Hometown School District to come to grips with its changing reality was creative tension generated by coming to grips with the brutal facts. The author of *The Fifth Discipline: The Art and Practice of the Learning Organization* (1990) and a leading expert in systems thinking, Peter Senge defines creative tension as the gap between our vision and reality. He explains that if there were no gap, there would be no need for any action to move toward our vision.

At Hometown Schools, school leaders and the community were very proud of their district's heritage of educational excellence and they didn't want to lose it. Confronting the brutal facts generated the creative tension that provided them with the will and the energy to meet the educational needs of their changing student body.

In his study to identify U.S. companies that have been able to make the leap from good to great, Jim Collins found that the ability and willingness to confront the brutal facts is one of the distinguishing characteristics of the 11 firms that accomplished this feat. These good-to-great companies reported that when you start with an honest and diligent effort to determine the truth of a situation, the right decisions often become self-evident.

These good-to-great companies worked diligently to create a corporate climate where the truth is heard and the brutal facts are confronted. The leaders of these companies understood that there is a huge difference between the opportunity to have your say and the opportunity to really be heard. What they did was create a corporate culture in which people were heard and, ultimately, where the truth was heard.

For educational leaders, the challenge is to resist the temptation to sugarcoat negative situations and, instead, confront the brutal facts head-on.

Key Thought

The brutal facts generate real answers.

CHAPTER 13

Become a Student of the Change Process

This may sound familiar. You are a building principal and the reading scores of your students are below standard. To solve the problem, you adopt a new reading program which has proven to be highly effective in other school districts. While some of your teachers are excited about it, others are not and oppose it.

After a year of struggling to implement the new program, you give up and go back to the old way of teaching reading. However, the reading scores continue to deteriorate and the resulting political pressure forces you to seek another assignment in the school system. In this case, rather than working for you, the change process worked against you.

There is a natural reluctance for change. We all know this. Even when change is positive, we often prefer maintaining the status quo.

Why is this and what can we do about it?

At a time in which the rate of change in our society seems to be outpacing our ability to adjust to it, this question is becoming increasingly relevant. In fact, a strong argument can be made that the pace of change in our public schools is now as great as, or greater than, it is in many other sectors.

Yet for a growing number of educational leaders the pace of change in our public schools may not be rapid enough. In their heart of hearts they are becoming fearful that our public school culture may not be able to change quickly enough to survive the growing social and political pressure that is closing in on it.

So how do you change a culture and the values and beliefs that drive it?

John P. Kotter, one of our nation's leading experts on the change process, has developed an eight-stage process of creating major change. One of his key points in *Leading Change* (1996) is that the change process doesn't begin with the culture. It ends there.

Kotter believes that the first step in the change process is establishing a sense of urgency. He explains that with complacency high, transformations usually go nowhere because few people are even interested in working on the change problem. Establishing a sense of urgency, he says, is crucial to gaining the needed cooperation.

The next six steps are:

2. Create a guiding coalition of key opinion leaders.
3. Develop a clear vision and strategy.
4. Communicate the change of vision.
5. Empower employees for broad-based action.
6. Generate short-term wins.
7. Consolidate gains and produce more change.

The final step of the change process, step 8, is to anchor new approaches in the culture. Changes can come undone, reminds Kotter, even after years of effort because the new approaches haven't been anchored firmly in group norms and values.

As an educational leader, change can work for you or against you. So, whether it is convincing a teaching staff to change what it teaches and how it teaches it or reminding a nation that saving our system of public schools is vitally important to our future, harnessing the power of the change process is a must.

Key Thought

Make the change process work for you
rather than against you.

CHAPTER 14

Have a Transition Plan

For many of you, the following story will strike a responsive chord.

Mary served as superintendent of a small suburban school district for eight years. During her time there, she instituted, without much fanfare, a number of important educational programs.

The first six years of her superintendency went as smoothly as glass. The school district budget was flush and student achievement was flourishing. Everyone and everything seemed to be on cruise control.

Then, without warning, the state initiated a series of deep budget cuts that threw her district's finances into turmoil. When her school board was forced to place a tax increase proposal on the ballot, a Pandora's box of past sins opened up and overflowed like the lava from a newly erupting volcano.

At the core of this lava flow was an incident that had occurred in 1963. The incident involved the demolition of a building that had served as the district's high school for nearly 35 years.

While many residents at the time had been very upset with the decision to demolish the old high school, it was now assumed that it was no longer an issue. Wrong.

The budget crisis and request for additional taxes resurrected this latent issue. As a result, the tax proposal was soundly defeated and the life of the superintendent went from six years of smooth sailing to two years of chaos in which everything that happened seemed to turn sour.

By the time Mary retired, she had become a scapegoat for the ills of the past and the present. In addition, much of what she had accomplished academically lost its luster.

So when it came time to hire her replacement, the school board decided the district needed a fresh start and named a superintendent who would bring new ideas and programs to the district and replace the old ones which had become tainted by their association with the former superintendent. And that is exactly what he did.

The phenomenon of throwing the baby out with the bathwater is all too common in our public schools. When we grow tired of someone or become disenchanted with them, we throw them out and bring in new blood. We also do this with our political leaders and with many of the products and services that we use.

However, in our public schools, we often pay a heavy price for it. We lose good programs and dilute others by adding one new exciting program after another. This is commonly called the flavor-of-the-month problem.

As the turnover of leaders and programs occurs, administrators and teachers develop a crying-wolf mindset and halfheartedly support the new programs that are in place because they know that they will be short-lived and eventually replaced.

While there are no quick and easy answers to the scenario that has just been painted, one thing is for certain. Without an effective transition plan, it is destined to occur over and over again.

During a period of leadership transition, which is usually the year prior to the main transition and the year following it, there is a window of opportunity to accomplish a number of important goals.

One is that you can drive into the school district culture what is working educationally so it doesn't get lost in the transition shuffle. You can also expose and defuse any skeletons from the past that are likely to reappear when things begin heating up.

Another opportunity that presents itself during a leadership transition period is to extend the honeymoon of the newly hired superintendent. By developing and implementing a year-long engagement strategy during the first year, the superintendent and board can create a strong base of support to counteract problems that will ultimately emerge down the road.

In this day and age, having a transition plan is not a luxury. It is a necessity.

Key Thought

Use transition periods as windows of opportunity
to preserve the best of the past
and secure the future.

CHAPTER 15

Teach What School Is Like Today

In my work with the public schools, I spend a lot of time in my car traveling from one school district to another. On average, I suppose I drive nearly 300 miles every day.

To help pass the time, I listen to talk radio. While I don't always agree with them, I enjoy hearing the viewpoints of the conservative talk show hosts who seem to do their homework on most discussion topics.

However, as intelligent and diligent as they seem to be, these powerful radio personalities appear to be unaware of what school is like today. They don't understand how school has changed during the past decade and how much progress is being made in many public school systems across our country.

Instead, they focus on conventional wisdom such as: The public schools are out of control, they focus too much on protecting the self-esteem of their students, and they cater to the at-risk population and don't challenge the brighter students. While this may be true in some public schools, it isn't that way everywhere and it isn't the direction in which our schools are headed.

As a result, old images of what school is like serve as the primary frame of reference for talk show hosts, school board members, and, for that matter, nearly everyone else. How teachers are teaching and students are learning in today's classroom is not well understood.

Instead, what most people know about going to school is based upon their personal experience of having gone to school or on media images of some of today's school-related problems.

The fact that most people have not made the transition from what school was like in the "good old days" to what it is like today is more than significant. It is potentially dangerous.

As long as citizens don't understand that teachers now truly have the ability—given enough time and the right tools—to "leave no child behind," they will continue to question the future viability of our system of public education. As long as they fail to see the real progress being made in public schools across America, they will continue to search for better educational alternatives.

The bottom line is simply this: One of the most important jobs of any educational leader is to teach others what school is like today. Whether it is your school board, parents, or a group of community leaders, sit them down with three or four of your best teachers and have a discussion about the great work being done in their classrooms.

Your citizens need to hear directly from those on the firing line that we finally know how to reach most children and help them learn. They need to know that we can identify individual learning styles and adapt teaching strategies to meet them.

For school administrators, teachers, and classroom aides, this is old news. However, for everyone else, it is brand-new information.

So, it is no wonder that there is a huge abyss between what the public schools are doing and what their communities think they are doing. In essence, they are like two ships passing in the night.

Key Thought

What we don't understand we often don't support.

CHAPTER 16

Delegate and Enforce Responsibility

For the past two years, staff morale in the district's one elementary building was on the rocks. It had reached the point where there were two distinct camps of teachers who would barely speak to one another.

Nearly every day, at least one teacher would end the day in tears. And to make matters worse, it was beginning to have a negative effect on teaching and learning.

The elementary principal was even more frustrated and concerned than the teaching staff. She had tried about everything to fix the problem. She had met with each teacher individually, spoken with her entire staff on numerous occasions, and brought in a conflict resolution expert. But nothing seemed to work.

So, in a desperate, last-ditch effort to break the logjam, she told all of her teachers to go into a room, close the door, and not come out until they had resolved their differences. They did it, and to her great surprise and delight, it worked.

The question is: Why did it work? The answer is that there are at least a couple of reasons.

One involves the work of Frederick Hertzberg. Regarded as one of this country's leading behavior scientists, he conducted a benchmark study in 1976 to determine what motivates people in the workplace.

In the study he compared factors such as achievement, recognition, company policy, salary, responsibility, advancement interpersonal relations, working conditions, and the work itself.

What he learned is that what motivates people for the longest period of time is giving them responsibility. The motivational staying power of the other factors lasted only a few days or weeks.

Another reason why the teachers stepped up and took care of their problem is that giving them the responsibility to solve it defused the psychological battle between their parent and child that was raging inside them and triggered the adult part of their psyches to step up and take charge.

In the early 1970s, a popular child psychologist and author by the name of Alfred Adler espoused the theory that within all of us there is a child, a parent, and an adult. Depending upon the situation, each of them is in charge of our psyche at any particular point in time.

Since our "child" tends to be self-centered, impatient, and immature and our "adult" tends to be bossy, controlling, and judgmental, many people problems are the result of "child-parent" conflicts.

One way to put our "adult" in charge is to give us responsibility. And that is exactly what the principal did.

Key Thought

When you give others responsibility,
they tend to act responsibly.

CHAPTER 17

Don't Treat Everyone the Same

The panel of presenters included four of the most highly respected teachers in the school district. Two represented the elementary staff, one the middle school, and the other the high school.

The audience for their presentation was a group of 25 business leaders from the community. Part of a statewide coalition of conservative political activists, these business leaders believed that the public schools were not doing their job and, as a result, the business leaders were supporting legislation to siphon money from the public schools for charter schools and vouchers.

The topic of the four presenters was "In School Today We No Longer Treat Everyone the Same." Each presenter shared how school has changed from the so-called "good old days." They talked about how they no longer lecture to students sitting in rows, how they are able to teach to individual learning styles, how important it is to work with pre-school children to get them on the right track, and how crucial it is to have reasonable class sizes in order to individualize instruction.

This explanation of what teachers do today in school and the message of hope and possibility caught the business leaders off guard. Prior to the presentation, their understanding of school focused on current images in the national media of problems in public schools and old images of their own experiences back when they were in school. They didn't have a clue about how far teaching and learning have come—especially during the past decade.

The irony of this story is that we don't practice what we preach when it comes to working with school employees. While we work to individualize teaching and learning for our students, we continue to fall into the trap of feeling we need to treat all of our school staff the same.

Whether it is salary schedules, staff development, or most other aspects of employee relations, we still treat our school staff like we used to treat our students. There is very little individualized evaluation and instruction for most educational teams.

In *First, Break All the Rules: What the World's Greatest Managers Do Differently* (1999), Marcus Buckingham and Curt Coffman point out that great managers don't treat everyone the same. They play favorites.

The two authors explain that although great managers are committed to the concept of fairness, in their mind "fairness" does not mean treating everyone the same. Rather, it means treating them as they deserve to be treated, bearing in mind what they have accomplished.

They add that if you spend the most time with your struggling performers and ignore your star performers, you can inadvertently alter the behavior of your stars. When you see them starting to slip, it is a sure sign that you've been paying attention to the wrong people and the wrong behaviors.

As a result, great managers invest in their best because it is extremely productive to do so and actively destructive to do otherwise. Great managers carve out a unique set of expectations that stretch and focus each particular individual, highlight and perfect each person's unique style, and run interference for each employee so that each one can maximize his or her talents.

Key Thought

Work with everyone but spend the most time developing your best people.

CHAPTER 18

Discover Carnegie's Secret

To hear him speak, he didn't sound very imposing. Napoleon Hill had a screechy, little voice that squawked like a chicken. And yet this man made one of the most important discoveries of our time.

As the story goes, one day Napoleon Hill, a respected college professor at Georgetown University in Washington, D.C., received an invitation from Andrew Carnegie, the famous steel magnate, to travel to Pittsburgh and meet with him at his home. Hill was among a hundred or so eminent scholars being interviewed by Carnegie for what ended up being a daunting task.

After three days of friendly conversation, Carnegie turned to Hill and asked him if he would be willing to spend the next 20 years of his life, and at his own expense, studying the lives of Thomas Edison, Henry Ford, Theodore Roosevelt, Orville and Wilbur Wright, and hundreds of other famous people whose achievements could be traced back to their association with Carnegie. Without hesitation, Hill accepted Carnegie's invitation to meet with them and discover the key to their great achievements.

After 20 years of research, Hill in 1937 unveiled in *Think and Grow Rich* why they were able to accomplish so much. He called it "Carnegie's secret," and he explained it this way.

He said that we become what we think about. He explained that we can literally take an idea and turn it into its physical equivalent—which is what Edison, Ford, and the others had done. It also is what my high school football team had done (see chapter 6).

Hill discovered that thoughts that are mixed with emotions constitute a magnetic force that attracts other similar or related thoughts. By planting a thought in our subconscious mind, we are able to tap into the combined intelligence of the universe.

We have all experienced to some degree or another the awesome power of our subconscious mind—like when an answer to a vexing problem suddenly appears from what seems to be the clear blue sky. We commonly think of it as inspiration.

What Carnegie's protégés did was utilize the power of the subconscious mind to focus on achieving a lifelong goal.

In addition to being an effective way to achieve goals, utilizing the power of Carnegie's secret—becoming what we think about—is a great way both to solve problems and to avoid them. By understanding that we become what we think about, we can think about things that we want to have happen as well as avoid thinking about things that we don't want to have happen.

Embedded within the culture of our schools and communities are a number of deeply rooted beliefs or things we think about that have influenced the thinking of educational leaders and that continue to serve as self-fulfilling prophecies. For example, today the term *public engagement* is becoming synonymous with a popular "new" strategy to gin up public support for the schools.

It is now politically correct for educational leaders to engage the community in making important decisions regarding the schools. However, this developing cultural belief can, and often does, create unintended side effects, and it occurs in a couple of ways.

First, in developing public engagement strategies, educational leaders often focus exclusively on the community and ignore their own school employees. Second, in bypassing their staff, they fail to frame the public discussion in a way that will include what is most important to most people—and that is the teaching and learning of children. Instead, the discussion often gets bogged down in political and financial issues that are unproductive and divisive.

So, what ends up happening in this public engagement process is the opposite of what you wanted to have happen. Instead of increasing public understanding and support, you create misunderstanding and decrease support.

Here are other strongly held and widely accepted beliefs that influence the thinking and actions of educational leaders: The longer you stay in one place, the more enemies you make; parents won't attend a school function unless you involve their children in it; we can do more with less; parents are too busy to get involved in the education of their children; creating blue-ribbon committees and other citizen task forces generates buy-in from the community; to increase public trust and support, we need to promote more of the good things that are happening in our schools; and it is not possible, politically speaking, to add the administrative support that is needed in our schools today.

These beliefs and others like them can become self-fulfilling prophecies that generate a wide range of unintended consequences. Some of these unintended consequences are discussed in the next chapter.

Key Thought

We become what we think about,
both as individuals and as organizations.

CHAPTER 19

Beware of Unintended Consequences

The more complex the situation, the more difficult it is to identify unintended consequences. For example, the pressure to be fiscally responsible in the current anti-tax climate forces school boards to place tax issues on the ballot before the money is really needed. They do this so that if the tax issue is not approved, they have another chance to get it passed before serious educational cuts have to be made.

In Ohio and probably in other states where school districts must rely on the passage of local tax issues to fund at least part of their operations, this is common practice. However, in trying to be responsible by asking for the money before it is really needed, what school officials are actually doing is triggering a chain reaction of negative side effects discussed below.

First, placing a tax issue on the ballot before it is needed makes it difficult, if not impossible, to establish a sense of urgency among voters. This, in turn, erodes public trust by creating a crying-wolf mindset when the issue is defeated and there are no visible consequences.

The lack of a clear sense or urgency then often leads to more tax issue proposals being placed on the ballot—whether or not the money is really needed—because school officials surmise that if they don't keep the proposal on the ballot, residents will feel that they didn't need the money in the first place. However, by continually asking voters to approve the tax issue, the No voters grow angrier with a "what-part-of-no-don't-you-understand" attitude, and they dig in their heels and work overtime to defeat any and all future tax issue proposals that come their way.

To complicate matters, the growing parade of tax issue attempts begins to wear down both school district employees and the citizens' committees that are working to pass them.

After a while, school officials grow weary of losing and decide to appease the No voters by freezing staff salaries, cutting athletics, eliminating busing, and making other cuts and reductions. But since No voters have an insatiable appetite for making cuts, these reductions only serve as "additional proof that the school district has more money than it needs."

Below are strongly held and widely accepted beliefs (discussed in the previous chapter) that influence the thinking and actions of educational leaders and the unintended consequences that they can generate.

"The longer you stay in one place, the more enemies you make." So, what often happens is that educational leaders never stay in one place long enough to get anything done, which weakens their ability to lead because everyone knows that they won't be around very long. In addition they and their family live a nomadic life, never staying in one place long enough to create strong roots.

"Parents won't attend a school function unless you involve their children in it." This belief severely limits the quality of meaningful communication that can occur with parents. For example, it excludes the opportunity to connect with parents by sitting down with them and simply talking about what is most important to them without using their children as a hook to get them to show up for the discussion.

"We can do more with less." At the root of this belief is the efficiency model that was discussed earlier in this book and which is embedded deeply within the culture of our educational system. The impact of believing and saying "we can do more with less" is that we create unrealistic expectations of ourselves and set ourselves up for failure. As a result, we push ourselves and our school employees beyond reasonable limits, fail to meet the educational needs of our students, and end up disappointing ourselves and others in our school district.

"Parents are too busy to get involved in the education of their children." The result of this belief is that we give up before we start and don't even try to get parents involved in the education of their children.

"Creating blue-ribbon committees and other citizen task forces generates buy-in from the community." While utilizing the expertise of the

community can be extremely helpful in framing important decisions, it is often not an effective public relations technique and does not always lead to buy-in and support from the public. In fact, it often backfires. Promoting these school-district task forces can send a not-so-subtle message to other residents in the community that their opinions don't matter.

"To increase public trust and support, we need to promote more of the good things that are happening in our schools." Real trust and support are created when we struggle together to solve problems that are important to us. Focusing only on the "good things" that are happening in our schools leads to distrust and lack of support because people know when they are being manipulated.

"It is not possible, politically speaking, to add the administrative support that is needed in our schools today." There is a big difference between spending money efficiently on what is really needed and wasting money on things that are not really needed. While it is true that most people are opposed to administrative bureaucracy and waste, they are not against providing their schools with the support that is needed.

The point being made here is reminiscent of the saying that you need to be careful about what you ask for because you may get it and end up not liking it. What may appear to be an obvious solution to a problem in the short run may end up unintentionally causing additional problems in the long run.

Key Thought

Some solutions create more problems
than they resolve.

CHAPTER 20

Study Quantum Theory

What Napoleon Hill didn't realize when he discovered Carnegie's secret (that we become what we think about) is that he had also discovered a brand-new world of power and possibility. It is called the quantum world.

If you go back and look at how our current views on humanity have evolved, you'll find they have evolved from the scientific positions we've taken. If you go back 200 or 300 years, the whole world was enamored with what is called Newtonian physics. In Newtonian physics, it was believed that life consisted of matter and its building blocks called atoms.

Now, with the discovery of quantum physics, scientists have taken these atoms that we used to think of as the tiniest particles of matter and have broken them down into subatomic particles. As they have broken them down into tiny subatomic particles, they've found that as we get to the tiniest particles, there are no more particles—that these particles are connected at the subatomic level by some kind of an invisible force that consists of pure energy.

Today, many of the leading thinkers in business, science, education, and other fields have reached the same conclusion: The universe does not operate the way Isaac Newton thought it did. They now believe that we do not live in a one-dimensional world of cause and effect but, instead, reside in one that consists of invisible subatomic building blocks of energy that organize the particles of matter that we can see.

Take, for example, the complex act of riding a bicycle. Once we learn how to ride a bike, we possess a knowing, not just a belief, that we can ride—even if it has been 30 years since we last rode. In addition, we still have the memory of how to ride in spite of the fact that the cells of our brain where the memories of how to ride a bike were stored 30 years ago are now gone. The cells all have changed, but the knowing is still there. Whatever the invisible intelligence, or pure awareness, was that allowed us to ride back then has somehow transcended our physicality.

Quantum physicists have discovered that this invisible intelligence consists of nonmaterial fields of energy that are created at the subatomic level by the energizing effect of information. They explain that information is more than mere content. It is the creative energy of the universe and it organizes matter into form.

Margaret Wheatley states in her seminal book *Leadership and the New Science: Learning about Organization from an Orderly Universe* (1990) that nothing exists at the subatomic level without engagement with another energy source. She explains that in the quantum world reality changes shape and meaning because of our activity—that we literally make it up as we go along.

For educational leaders, three important implications of this discussion about the quantum world are as follows:

- There is a solution (or are solutions) to all problems.
- Lasting solutions with positive side effects must grow out of a process of engagement where people sit down together and share their energy (i.e., work things out).
- Off-the-shelf solutions to problems are not directly transferable to new situations but can serve as starting points for creating the unique solutions that are needed.

Key Thought

Studying quantum theory will help you
see problems in a different light
and generate solutions that
previously didn't exist.

CHAPTER 21

Teach Yourself to Think Like Peter Senge

From a very early age, we've been taught that every cause has an effect. If we do A, then B will occur.

However, what we have not been taught to do is see the long-term effects of doing A. What's more, as was discussed in chapter 19, the long-term effects may be quite different from what we intended to have happen.

In *The Fifth Discipline: The Art and Practice of the Learning Organization* (1990), Peter Senge explains that events actually occur in patterns and these patterns have a life of their own and control outcomes. By understanding the patterns that shape behavior, we can identify actions that, in many instances, are feeding our problems and causing us to fail.

The discipline of identifying these patterns is called *systems thinking.* One of the world's leading authorities in the newly emerging field of systems thinking, Senge has identified certain patterns that occur again and again. He calls these recurring patterns the "laws of systems thinking."

Here are a few examples of these laws:

Today's problems come from yesterday's solutions. We are often puzzled by the causes of our problems, but remembering solutions to past problems provides insight. For instance, why are educators struggling to reduce class sizes? One answer is because efficiency experts convinced them in the early 1900s that increasing class sizes would make their schools more efficient and save them money.

The cure can be worse than the disease. What seems at first glance to be the obvious solution is sometimes not just ineffective but also dangerous. Eliminating educational programs to balance the school district budget, for example, not only masks the need for more money but also lowers the quality of education and can trigger a long-term process of dismantling educational programs.

Faster is slower. All natural systems, ecosystems, or organizations have an optimal rate of growth that is far slower than the fast pace most of us think is desirable. For instance, the current drive to reform our public schools is running headlong into the natural tendency for people to adjust slowly to change.

Cause and effect are not closely related in time and space. The first step in learning how to view reality systemically is to dispense with simple cause-and-effect thinking and learn to see that often we, not external adversaries or events, are at the root of our problems. For instance, trying to convince residents to feel good about their schools can in the long run lead to public distrust because these residents over time may feel they are being manipulated.

The harder you push, the harder the system pushes back. We have all felt it. The more you try to improve things, the more effort is required. For instance, the harder you try to convince some teachers that they need to improve upon their teaching methods, the more they resist and the harder it is to get them to change.

Key Thought

Recognizing the patterns that shape behavior
gives you the power (or leverage) to change them.

CHAPTER 22

Stop Trying to Make Everyone Feel Good

One day, an old man, a young boy, and their donkey were entering the outskirts of a small village. As the young boy led the donkey and its rider, the old man, down the main street of town, a group of five or six people who happened to notice the threesome began to mutter: "It is unfair that the old man gets to ride and the young boy has to walk."

Well, the young boy and old man overheard these critical comments and, feeling the pressure to respond to the comments from this small group of bystanders, decided to trade places. So the old man got off the donkey and the young boy got on and they continued their journey through town.

After a couple of blocks, the old man and the young boy passed another group of five or six people who, too, began to mutter: "It is unfair that the young boy gets to ride and the old man has to walk."

At this point, the pressure was really getting to both the young boy and old man. After pondering what to do, the two decided they both would ride the donkey to avoid additional criticism. So, with the two on its back, the donkey took a few steps and then keeled over and died because of all the added weight.

As you might surmise, there is a valuable moral to this story, and it is this: When you try to please all of the people all of the time, you lose your you-know-what.

If you are an educational leader or thinking about becoming one, you need to take this story to heart because the culture of your profession nurtures the belief that educational leaders must try to please everyone, and passes this belief on—from one generation of educational leaders to another. Trying to make people feel good is what educational leaders are taught to do from the first day on the job.

While trying to make others feel good is not necessarily a bad thing to do, it can create a web of negative unintended consequences. Take, for example, the widely held belief that to increase public support for our schools, we need to publicize more of the good things that we are doing.

In trying to make others feel good about what we are doing in our schools, we inadvertently mislead them by not telling them the whole story. In addition to eroding trust and confidence, this creates a false sense of security and makes it very difficult to create the level of urgency required to energize "the choir" to drive important changes that need to be made. (Note: I will talk more about energizing the choir in Chapter 26.)

Blinded by the need to make everyone feel good about our public schools, we have not taken the time to sit down with school boards, parents, community leaders, and others and clearly spell out how much educational capacity we need today to educate all students. In fact, we complicate matters by focusing public attention on our positive test scores and creating the illusion that all is well while students continue to fall through the educational cracks.

So instead of pointing out the shortcomings that need to be addressed in order to increase our educational capacity, we plod along doing the best that we can. We continue to accept more responsibility for educating more children, we learn more about how we can educate them, and then we become frustrated by the lack of time, staff, and energy to do it. Ironically, we do all of this while smiling and telling everyone that everything is okay.

The bottom line is that we should stop trying to please others to make them feel good about us and our schools. Instead, as was discussed in Chapter 3, we should treat them with the kind of respect, openness, and honesty that we ourselves want and deserve.

Key Thought

*While feel-good strategies may work in the short run,
they often generate negative, unintended consequences
in the long run.*

CHAPTER 23

Sell Problems Rather Than Solutions

Growing up, my brother and I lived in a small town north of Dayton, Ohio. It was an Ozzie-and-Harriet type of community—"a good place to raise children."

In our backyard was a shallow ravine that many years before had housed the track of a streetcar line that carried West Milton residents to Dayton and home again. On the other side of the ravine lived twin boys who we less-than-affectionately called "the river rats." I'll get back to them in a minute.

As siblings are prone to do, my brother Mike and I would periodically get into skirmishes. I vividly remember one incident when we were painting our bicycles and I tricked him into shaking up a quart of black paint after I had loosened the lid. Yes, you guessed it—half of the paint ended up all over his face and hair.

Mike, of course, had his way of getting back at me. In addition to being a prolific biter, he would go after me wildly flailing his cap gun with the goal of doing me bodily harm. Being two-and-a-half years older, I ran faster than he did and usually was able to escape his wrath.

While it was okay for Mike and me to go at it, that unwritten rule didn't apply to the outside world. This was especially true when it came to the river rats on the other side of our ravine. Whenever these twin bullies would pick on Mike, I would lose it. I would literally go into a rage and, although I don't consider myself to be a person who goes searching for opportunities to get into a fight with someone, I'd react to the crisis at hand and go after them to protect my younger brother.

My behavior was not unique. It is part of the fabric of our nation. While we can fight among ourselves about trivial issues and concerns, as Americans we will rise to the occasion and pull together when facing a real crisis.

For example, after the terrorist attacks on 9-11, what had seemed so important prior to that fateful day suddenly disappeared—at least temporarily. Our national pastime, major league baseball, was even put on hold while we mourned the loss of thousands of lives and the loss of innocence for our way of life.

Yes, as a people we will fight among ourselves over sports, politics, and other mundane issues. However, when a real crisis hits, we'll pull together faster than a bolt of lightning on a hot summer evening. The sense of urgency created by a crisis wakes us up and helps put into proper perspective what is really important and what is not so important.

In *Leading Change* (1996), John Kotter writes that establishing a sense of urgency is crucial to gaining needed cooperation. He explains that with complacency high, transformations usually go nowhere because few people are even interested in working on the change problem. He adds that increasing urgency demands that we remove sources of complacency or minimize their impact.

One of the reasons why educational leaders create problems for themselves is that they are taught to do the opposite of what John Kotter preaches. Rather than exposing an existing sense of urgency to help pull people together to work through problems and generate change, educators (as was addressed in prior chapters) are in the habit of hiding or ignoring problems or of putting positive spins on them.

Even in situations where the problem cannot be ignored or spun in a positive way, the typical strategy utilized by many educational leaders is to work out a solution as quickly as possible and then sell it to the staff, parents, community, or whomever.

The problem with selling quick solutions, however, is that more often than not we end up selling the solution to people who don't fully understand the problem being resolved. As a result, the proposed solution becomes a source of contentiousness and those who must live with it begin bickering over whether or not it is the right solution.

This bickering, then, leads to what is called a "solution war." Going to a block schedule, expanding the school day, making changes in how student progress is measured and reported, requesting a tax increase, and redistricting enrollment patterns are all solutions that can be very divisive if the reasons why these changes need to be made are not clearly understood.

Unfortunately, as a society, we have become experts at selling solutions. We create financial oversight boards, blue-ribbon committees, and other specialized task forces to legitimize what we do so we can better sell whatever we feel needs to get done. We even publish special newsletters or place inserts in local newspapers to sell solutions to problems that are not clearly understood.

For example, instead of explaining the fact that lack of space is creating large class sizes and limiting course offerings (the core problem), we try to sell the features of a new building (the solution to the core problem).

The bottom line is that the clearer the problem, the clearer the sense of urgency. And the clearer the sense of urgency, the easier it is to arrive at a solution that makes the most sense for the situation at hand. In fact, there is usually a clear-cut solution to every problem, once the problem is clearly understood.

Like 9-11 and the times when my brother was picked on by the twin bullies, many of the current problems faced by educational leaders provide an opportunity to generate a sense of urgency and pull people together to work through situations and get things done.

Key Thought

By selling problems rather than solutions,
you can create the sense of urgency required
to clarify needs and bring people together
to work through issues and concerns
and create positive change.

CHAPTER 24

Focus on Tactics

During the war in Iraq, General Tommy Franks referred to the overall military strategy as being one of speed and flexibility. Many in the news media who covered the war were confused, if not frustrated, by this strategy because they didn't fully understand it.

They expected our military leaders to report on concrete and sequential action steps planned in advance and rigidly followed. (Once our troops reach point A, they will go to point B and then to point C and so on.) However, a "speed and flexibility" strategy was something quite different.

For example, while the American public was told by the news media that a "shock and awe" strategy would be the first step in the military campaign, it didn't happen. Instead, a tactical strike was undertaken in an attempt to take out Saddam Hussein.

Rather than focusing on a few grand strategies written in stone, our military leaders focused on tactics during the war in Iraq. These tactics were developed along the way after strategies were introduced, the realities of specific situations emerged, and effective adjustments could be made. These adjustments were the tactics.

In a sense, it was like building an airplane on the fly. While military strategists could theorize about what to do, it wasn't until their troops reached a destination and saw what was really happening that they could figure their next best action step.

In school districts across America, educational leaders have bought into the idea that strategy is king. They have spent huge blocks of time and, in some cases, significant sums of money to build elaborate strategies to improve teaching and learning.

Unfortunately, many of these strategies are sitting on shelves waiting to be fully implemented. The initial energy that drove the planning process just seems to dissipate.

Then, to complicate matters, some school districts try to revive their strategic plan by turning it into a total quality plan, a continuous improvement plan, a Baldrige initiative, or all of the above.

In 1984, *Business Week* reviewed the history of the strategic plans of 33 major companies and found that 19 had failed. While this may not have signaled the end of the infatuation of business with strategic planning, it certainly contributed to a clearer understanding of the limitations of the strategic planning process.

Today, in successful companies, tactics drive strategies as much as or more than strategies drive tactics. While strategies are built upon a perception of what reality is likely to be, tactics are built upon the reality of what it is.

The following is a good example of why educational strategies require effective tactics in order to make them work.

A team of teachers, administrators, and community members are sent to a national workshop to evaluate a popular strategic planning process that has achieved dramatic success in some high-profile school districts. When they return to their district, they convince educational leaders to adopt the new planning process and then spend the next six months drafting a plan that will lead their school system to the same destination as the high-profile school districts they saw at the national workshop.

At the heart of the district's newly developed strategic plan is the need to restructure grade levels, which means moving some teachers to different buildings. While this strategy makes sense on paper, it isn't until it is tested in the field that it becomes real.

And the reality is that some of the teachers are opposed to the idea. Comfortable with the status quo, they are especially concerned about having to leave some of their friends.

In this scenario, the tactics employed to help the teaching staff work through the anxiety of moving to new buildings will drive the district's strategy to restructure grade levels. These tactics, in turn, will grow out of meaningful discussions with the teachers affected by the proposed changes.

While developing on-the-ground tactics to implement general strate-gies makes sense, and it worked for our military leaders in Iraq and continues to work for many successful companies, the idea of focusing on tactics is not yet embedded in the mindset of the culture of public education. Until it is, unfortunately, many well-developed strategic plans will continue to sit on shelves gathering dust.

Key Thought

Tactics drive strategies as much as or more than strategies drive tactics.

CHAPTER 25

Realize That Little Things
Can Make a Big Difference

The stakes were high. If the school tax levy didn't pass, it meant a significant number of layoffs and severe cuts in educational services.

As the 100 or so campaign workers and other school supporters nervously awaited the phone call from the local board of elections, the tension was almost unbearable. With only a 12-vote lead, the outcome of the election still was very much in doubt.

Then, the phone rang. Within a matter of a few seconds, the hope that had provided the energy for one of the most effective grassroots campaigns in the school district's history turned into disappointment, disillusionment, and anger. Everyone in the room not only felt rejected but also believed they had let their schools and community down.

When the local newspaper reporter asked the school board president why she thought the tax issue was defeated, the president's comments reflected what everyone was feeling: "We worked hard to educate our community about the need for this tax levy. As a result of the defeat, there are going to be major consequences that will impact negatively on our teachers and students."

When asked what would be the next step, the board president said, "We are going to put the issue back on the ballot as soon as possible and try to do a better job of selling it to the voters."

Although they didn't seem to be that significant at the time, the quotes of the board president had a deep and lasting impact on the residents of the school district. And it wasn't positive.

The angry and revengeful tone of what was said spread like wildfire. It was the major topic of discussion in hair salons, grocery stores, restaurants, and other meeting places throughout the school district.

As a result, not only did voters defeat the following two tax proposals, but they also replaced the board president at the next school board election.

For school districts that have to rely on local tax elections for financial support, this story is a familiar scenario. In Ohio, for example, there are about 200 school district tax issues on the ballot every May and every November.

The lesson to be learned from the story is that little things (like quotes in the newspaper) can mean more than just a lot. They can mean everything.

Little things can have an impact that grows out of control and consumes the community grapevine.

Malcolm Gladwell calls this phenomenon the *tipping point*—the dramatic moment when everything can change all at once. It is the moment of critical mass, the threshold, the boiling point.

He explains in *The Tipping Point: How Little Things Can Make a Big Difference* (2000) that the context in which an event occurs, an action takes place, or words are spoken can have a powerful impact on the way in which it is received and how far it is spread. The convictions of your heart and the actual contents of your thoughts, he asserts, are less important, in the end, than the immediate context in which they play out.

The context in this situation was an emotionally charged atmosphere following the narrow defeat of an important school tax election. With public attention strongly focused upon the board president's comments, her seemingly insignificant quotes for the newspaper reporter spread like an epidemic throughout her school district.

So while what you say may sometimes seem to be of little consequence, it may mean everything within the context in which you say it.

Key Thought

Be careful what you say because
more people than you think may be listening.

CHAPTER 26

Turn the Choir into Your Offensive Line

How many times have we been told that we shouldn't waste our time preaching to the choir—to those individuals who we feel are already on our side and will support how we think and what we do? As a result of the widespread belief that we shouldn't waste our time preaching to the choir, the choir tends to be either taken for granted and ignored or fed a constant diet of good news to keep it comfortable and happy.

In both instances, the consequence is the same. These strategies put the choir to sleep. However, when preaching to the choir embodies urgency, motivation, and empowerment, it can inspire action. In this sense, not only is preaching to the choir a productive activity, it is essential if those in our society who believe in the importance of fostering the common good are to control their destiny.

An empowered choir is like an offensive line in football that opens holes for its running backs to gain yardage and protects the quarterback from getting sacked. For educational leaders, the choir consists of a significant cross section of fellow administrators, teachers, school board members, students, parents, civic leaders, and the community as a whole.

One quick example will illustrate how you can turn the choir into your offensive line.

The story is true and involves a construction project at a high school building nestled in the middle of a well-established residential neighborhood. In doubling the size of the high school, construction project crews and their big, noisy, dust-generating equipment were about to invade this quiet neighborhood.

In this instance, the "choir" consisted of a large segment of the neighborhood residents who were usually supportive of the local schools. However, as concern about the project spread, some nonsupportive residents began to work the rumor mill with negative misinformation.

In order to turn them (the choir) into the offensive line for the school board and administration, the following steps were taken to ease the concerns of residents in the neighborhood and to provide them with accurate information. During the first few weeks of the project, the school district's community relations director walked the neighborhood and spoke informally with residents.

She asked questions such as, "What are your concerns about the project? How is your life and your home being affected by it? What can we do to ease your frustration and make the situation livable?"

In addition to having personal conversations with neighborhood residents, she published a weekly newsletter that included updates on the project—including information about what was coming next in the construction process. Finally, before the new high school officially opened, neighborhood residents were invited to take V.I.P. tours of the facility.

As a result of the neighborhood visits, weekly newsletter, and V.I.P. tours, school officials were able to turn the choir of neighborhood residents within earshot of the high school into their offensive line. With their help, school leaders were able to defuse negative feelings about the building project and turn many residents in the neighborhood into strong advocates for the school system.

For educational leaders, a strong offensive line composed of energized choir members is paramount when facing controversy or change.

Key Thought

When the "choir" doesn't help drive important decisions,
others will twist the intent of these decisions
and turn them against you.

CHAPTER 27

Put the Power of the Grapevine to Work

In 1952, on the island of Koshima, scientists who had observed Japanese monkeys in the wild for more than thirty years were providing them with sweet potatoes dropped in the sand. The monkeys liked the taste of the sweet potatoes, but they found the dirt unpleasant.

An 18-month-old female named Imo found that she could solve the problem by washing the potatoes in a nearby stream and taught this trick to her mother. Her playmates also learned this new way and they taught their mothers, too.

Between 1952 and 1958, all of the young monkeys learned to wash the sandy sweet potatoes to make them more palatable. Only the adults who imitated their children learned this social improvement. Other adults kept eating the dirty sweet potatoes.

Then something startling took place.

In the autumn of 1958, a certain number of Koshima monkeys were washing sweet potatoes. The exact number is not known. Let us suppose that when the sun rose one morning there were 99 monkeys on Koshima Island who had learned to wash their sweet potatoes. Let's further suppose that later that morning, the hundredth monkey learned to wash potatoes.

By that evening almost every monkey in the tribe was washing sweet potatoes before eating them. The added energy of this hundredth monkey had somehow created an ideological breakthrough.

To the great surprise of the scientists, the habit of washing sweet potatoes then jumped over the sea. Colonies of monkeys on other islands and the mainland began washing their sweet potatoes.

The important lesson to be learned from this discovery is that when the level of awareness reaches a critical mass point, it is picked up by nearly everyone within an energy field. That energy field can be a group of Japanese islands or it can be your school district.

The story of the hundredth monkey is also the story of the grapevine effect and how you as an educational leader can put the power of the grapevine to work in your school or school district. During your educational career, there will be many opportunities to utilize this power.

These opportunities may be narrow and impact only the nonteaching staff in one building, for example, or they may be broad and affect an entire school district. Below are examples of situations where the grapevine effect can help create long-term consensus around a potentially divisive issue:

- contemplating block scheduling
- reducing large class sizes
- raising teacher salaries
- dismissing a principal or teacher
- changing the student dress code
- trying to pass a school tax issue
- hiring a new superintendent
- consolidating school bus pickup points
- addressing concerns about outcome-based education
- raising student test scores
- restoring trust and confidence after a teacher strike
- increasing parent involvement
- closing a school building
- launching a strategic planning process
- expanding course offerings
- increasing graduation requirements

So, you may ask, what is the grapevine effect? Well, it is what everyone is talking about, the feeling out there, the word on the street, and the talk of the town. These are expressions that describe what is commonly known as the grapevine effect.

The community grapevine is not a figment of our imagination. It is real and can be explained scientifically. The grapevine effect occurs when the subatomic particles in a field of information grow and intensify to the point where they reach what is called a critical mass.

When this critical mass point is reached, the particles in the field of information suddenly become energized and, like a magnetic force, attract other particles to line up in the same way. This magnetized field of information then spreads like a wave throughout a teaching staff, group of parents, or school district.

In *The Power of Public Engagement: A Beacon of Hope for America's Schools* and *Putting the Power of Public Engagement to Work for Your Schools and Community* (both by William G. O'Callaghan, 1999), the process of creating a point of critical mass is discussed in great detail. The short version of the explanation, however, is that when a small group of people get involved in a discussion that is important to them, the information being discussed can reach a point of critical mass and become part of the collective consciousness of a much larger group of people.

See figure 27.1 for a graphic illustration showing how reaching a point of critical mass and creating the grapevine effect can work in a school district.

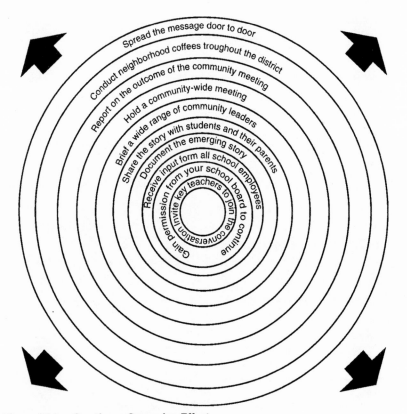

Figure 27.1. · *Creating a Grapevine Effect*

Like planting seeds and waiting for them to germinate, creating the grapevine effect also takes time—sometimes a year or more—and it requires patience while people work through various issues and concerns. As the following story illustrates, school officials in Medina, Ohio, understand how time-consuming it can be.

With student enrollment increasing at breakneck speed for several years, the Medina City School District was struggling with the decision of whether to add onto the current high school or build a second high school. For nearly two years, one-high-school-proponents were pitted against those who wanted two. However, that one "right answer" continued to elude everyone.

Then it suddenly became apparent that the issue was not simply about buildings. It was also about values.

Following this realization, school officials decided to put an idea on the table that represented what they felt was the majority opinion in the community. Fifty meetings were scheduled with community members in their homes to talk about the plan.

In two months, the school board and superintendent talked with more than 500 community members and what they heard was that the plan was not acceptable. However, as a result of these discussions, school officials were able to identify the core values that their community held regarding the high school building project.

From these core values, they were able to craft a solution that was discussed during the next few months in more than 100 additional neighborhood coffees.

When the dust settled, the energy of the choir of school district employees and residents in Medina who shared the goal of providing their children with a high quality education had finally reach a critical mass point. The power of the grapevine then took it from there—spreading the word throughout the school district that this solution made sense and should be adopted.

Key Thought

Building consensus through the power
of the grapevine is a step-by-step process
that can be shaped and controlled.

CHAPTER 28

Create a Crisis to Eliminate Deadwood

Janice had just been hired as the director of curriculum by a small school district in the rural part of the state to implement a newly created school reform plan. The product of a year of intense study, the plan was state-of-the-art and required the staff to rethink what they taught and how they taught it.

Energized by her new position and excited about the opportunity to revolutionize teaching and learning in this sleepy little school district, Janice hit the ground running. To sharpen her focus before the start of school, she even found time to attend a weeklong workshop on the latest school reform trends and techniques.

There was, however, a serious fly in the ointment. Many of the teachers were not involved in creating the school reform plan and saw no reason for it. Some, in fact, felt the plan was a slap in the face. It said to them that they weren't good enough and needed to change.

So, you guessed it—Janice and her exciting new ideas hit a brick wall. Not only was she unable to convince her teachers to adopt her changes, but she ultimately became a target for their anger and was forced to move to another school district within two years.

Asking people to change is difficult. Most of us are comfortable with the status quo and naturally resist the call to see and do things differently—especially when we are *told* we have to do it. And as many educational leaders have discovered in recent years, the aversion to change is deeply embedded in the public school culture.

With this reality ever present, what can Janice and others like her do to generate change? The ecocycle of a forest provides valuable insight for addressing this common challenge.

In its early stages of life, a forest abounds with vegetation as the direct sunlight generates life for thousands of species of plants. However, as the canopy of the forest thickens and sunlight to the floor is gradually shut out, fewer and fewer plants are able to survive and what is left is an increasing amount of deadwood.

For a mature forest to be renewed, it must first be destroyed. David K. Hurst, the author of *Crisis & Renewal: Meeting the Challenge of Organizational Change* (1995), calls this "creative destruction."

For educational leaders, creating a crisis and causing destruction run counter to their professional culture, which focuses on making others feel good and avoids negative occurrences such as crises. In fact, most educators spend a significant amount of their time trying to defuse crises, not create them.

Eliminating deadwood, whether it is vegetation in a forest or outdated ideas in a school system, sometimes requires the creation of a crisis. Just as a forest fire renews vegetation in its ecological system, a student achievement crisis in a school district that doesn't meet minimum academic standards can renew teaching and learning.

For Janice, what needed to occur in her newly adopted school system was for the state to announce that her district was not meeting educational standards and would not receive all of its state funding until improvements were made. This would have generated a trickle-down effect through her school board, superintendent, building principals, and teachers and would have created the crisis Janice needed to motivate her teachers to renew their commitment to meet the changing educational needs of their students.

Key Thought

*The energy generated by a crisis
provides the impetus for
change and renewal.*

CHAPTER 29

Understand How Power Has Shifted

It is amazing to observe. Within the brief time span of a generation, some of our nation's, and indeed the world's, most powerful institutions and professions have seen their dominance decline.

For example, in 1989, the entire world watched awe struck as the empire of the Soviet Union suddenly came unglued. Today, there is no Soviet Union—only remnants of it. Also, for decades, General Motors was regarded as the world's premier manufacturing company. Today, GM is struggling.

The fate of one of our most powerful professions underscores the extent of how power has shifted in our society.

Until recently, medical doctors in the United States were white-coated gods who virtually controlled the entire American health care system. Their personal and political clout was enormous.

Today, physicians are under siege from the insurance industry, managed care groups, the government, and their own nurses and patients. The knowledge monopoly of the medical profession has been thoroughly smashed.

As Alvin Toffler states in *Powershift: Knowledge, Wealth, and Violence at the Edge of the 21st Century* (1990), this case of the dethroned doctor is only one example of a more general process changing the entire relationship of knowledge to power in the high-tech nations of the world. In many other fields, the closely held knowledge of specialists is slipping out of control and reaching ordinary citizens.

And as knowledge is redistributed, so, too, is the power based on it.

This shift in power from large institutions to the individual citizen is not limited to the Soviet Union, GM, and the medical profession. There

was also a time in our country when the words of local mayors, minis-
ters, and school superintendents were golden and accepted without
question. Back in those days, public opinion could be shaped by one
powerful personality in a community, and it often was.

Fortunately or unfortunately—depending upon one's point of
view—those days of blind trust and loyalty are long gone. That bygone
era has been replaced by a healthy and sometimes not-so-healthy skep-
ticism of all our major public and private institutions and those who are
trying to lead them.

As a result of the eroding level of public trust and the increasing
amount of information available through modern technology, public
opinion is formed very differently today than it was even a generation
ago. It is no longer solely top-down but it is also bottom-up from the
grass roots.

For many school administrators who, like their counterparts in other
American institutions, have historically been revered by most citizens,
this shift in power comes as a great shock. Trust and respect are no
longer inherently built into an educational leader's job description.
These two attributes must be earned.

Today, the real source of power for educational leaders is through
their ability to engage their fellow administrators, teachers, students,
parents, school board members, community leaders, and other school
district residents. It is no longer a part of the institutional authority that
once existed.

Key Thought

*Rather than who you are or the position
you hold, it is your ability to energize others
that gives you the power to make a difference.*

CHAPTER 30

Learn How Public Decisions Are Really Made

The way public decisions are really made is not a lot different than buying a new car. You go online and find the make and model of the car you want and what it really costs. You then go out and visit dealerships so you can sit in the car, take a test drive, and begin negotiating for the best price.

All of this takes time, but you're in no hurry to sign on the dotted line until everything feels just right.

In his introduction to the Harwood Group's *Meaningful Chaos: How People Form Relationships with Public Concerns* (1993), Kettering Foundation President David Mathews states that two conditions are necessary for authentic public opinion to develop. The first is time for the public to grapple with what is really happening. Second, there must be open discussion in which the public carefully weighs the pros and cons of each issue.

This sounds very similar to buying a new car, doesn't it?

In this Kettering Foundation study, a number of factors that determine how public decisions are made and which challenge the conventional wisdom of educational leaders were identified. For example, the prevailing belief is that most people act purely in their self-interest. The study, however, found that people form relationships to public concerns often through a broader context beyond just "What's in it for me?"

Here are some more findings that provide important insight for educational leaders into how public decisions are really made:

- Although efforts to engage people on public concerns often place a premium on deluging them with facts, figures, and other information, people seek a deeper sense of understanding and meaning that enables them to see the "big picture."
- People resist polarization on public concerns. They seek, instead, room for ambivalence in which to question, discuss, and test ideas and gain confidence about their views.
- People desire a level of authenticity that rings true to them and gives them the feeling that they are being squared with.
- Everyday Americans, not just experts, are key catalysts in helping people form relationships with public concerns. Family members, friends, and neighbors often have a strong influence on how public decisions are made.

Daniel Yankelovich, in *Coming to Public Judgment: Making Democracy Work in a Complex World* (1991), explains that as observers in human psychology know well, all change is difficult—no matter how slight or great. When people are caught in cross pressures, before they can resolve them, it is necessary to struggle with the conflicts and ambivalences and defenses they arouse.

Yankelovich cautions that change requires hard work and rarely does it take place smoothly. Rather, it is full of backsliding, procrastination, and avoidance.

On any issue, the public must resolve where it stands cognitively, emotionally, and morally. Citizens must clarify fuzzy thinking, reconcile inconsistencies, and grasp the consequences of various choices, confront their own ambivalent feelings, and struggle with the impulse to put themselves and their own needs and desires ahead of their ethical commitment to do the right thing.

Like buying a new car, engaging the public in making decisions can take a lot of time and patience. On major issues, it may take a year or more for citizens to work through their concerns and become comfortable with things.

Think of it as planting seeds, feeding them, and giving them time to grow. This is how educational leaders need to lead their staffs and the

public through the decision-making process when facing important issues and concerns.

Key Thought

When making an important decision,
the public needs to be given time to work through
its impact and become comfortable with it.

CHAPTER 31

Build Strategies to Eliminate Barriers

If you're an elementary teacher in most school systems in this country, you have little if any quality time during the school day to interact with your peers or participate in professional development activities. Because of the way school has been organized over the years, the time to reflect, plan, and learn is usually relegated to after school, on the weekends, or during the summer.

To make a long story short: An enterprising administrator from a small school system on the shores of Lake Erie did something about the problem. Following nearly a year of in-depth discussion and careful planning with his teachers and administrators, he introduced a unique teacher assistant program using school district residents to free up time during the school day for his elementary staff to participate in professional development activities.

During that first year, he had an opportunity to address a number of barriers that, had they not been eliminated, would have prevented his idea to free up time for his teachers from getting off the ground.

Within a few months, his idea had turned into an effective solution to the lack-of-quality-time problem that had plagued his elementary staff. He and his school district even received statewide recognition and, as a result, he received many phone calls from other educational leaders who wanted to replicate the program in their districts. However, much to their chagrin, their efforts often fell flat.

Unlike the creator of the teacher assistant program, what these other educators failed to do was first take the time to identify and eliminate the barriers that were standing in the way. These barriers included the fact that building principals already have a lot on their plates and may not be too excited about another project—even when that project is a good one. In addition, many teachers do not feel comfortable leaving their classes with another person—even though they desperately seek more time during the day to collaborate with their peers and develop themselves professionally.

And then there is the issue of change. Even when change is positive, it creates stress for those involved in the change process.

In many schools today, a great amount of time and energy are devoted to developing and implementing educational improvement programs. However, within the culture of school administration, creating strategies to eliminate the barriers to educational improvement is a relatively foreign idea. As a result, ideas that work in one classroom or one building often remain there and never see the light of day in neighboring classrooms or buildings.

Hank Healey at North Carolina's Research Triangle Institute identified the reason why it is so difficult to scale up and sustain school reform. What he concluded from his research of the educational system in South Africa is that just as it is important to develop educational strategies to improve teaching and learning, it is also necessary to build strategies to remove the barriers that limit the capacity of schools to make these educational strategies available to all children.

So, what are the barriers preventing educational leaders from scaling up and sustaining school reform initiatives? Utilizing Dr. Healey's conceptual model, we have identified a number of these barriers, which are listed in figure 31.1.

In reality, these barriers do not act alone but work in tandem. However, any one of them can spell doom for nurturing a good idea and giving it life.

Key Thought

Identify barriers that are getting in your way
and create strategies to eliminate them.

Barriers to Educational Improvement
Why generating and sustaining change in our schools is so difficult

The Barrier Bubble

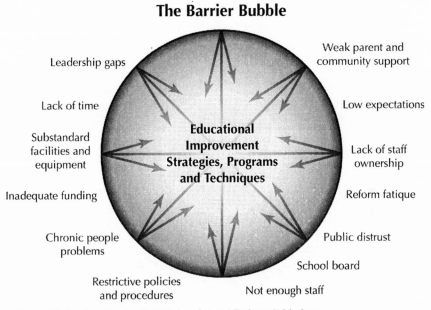

Figure 31.1. *Barriers to Sustaining School Reform Initiatives*

CHAPTER 32

Heed the Advice of Flight Attendants

If you have ever flown, you've probably heard the following announcement: "If cabin pressure changes, the panels above your seat will open, revealing oxygen masks. Reach up and pull a mask toward you, put it over your nose and mouth, and secure it with the elastic band that can be used to adjust the mask. The plastic bag will not fully inflate although oxygen is flowing."

Now, for the key point: "Remember to secure your own mask before helping others."

This advice from airline fight attendants prior to every departure reminds us that if we don't first take care of ourselves (in this instance, secure our own mask before helping others), we won't be much good to anyone else. In a profession in which the magnitude of the job sometimes appears to be overwhelming, it is easy for educational leaders to get caught up amid a growing list of responsibilities and become physically and emotionally drained.

In *The Seven Habits of Highly Effective People* (1989), Stephen Covey uses the fable of the goose and the golden egg to stress the need for self-renewal. He warns that if you don't keep the goose that lays the golden eggs healthy, it will eventually stop laying golden eggs.

Likewise, if you don't take care of yourself, you won't be able to provide the caliber of educational leadership that is both expected and needed. However, in a profession that seems to thrive on the stress associated with the job, many school administrators take pride in the fact that their job is so demanding and all consuming.

Sometimes it appears that job satisfaction among educational leaders is directly correlated with professional burnout. The more tired, frustrated, and overwhelmed they are, the more they seem to think they are meeting the expectations of their job.

For many educational leaders, taking care of themselves receives only lip service. The common refrain is that "we know we need to renew ourselves but we just don't have the time to do it."

In this day and age, however, this excuse is neither workable nor acceptable for leaders who are being asked to navigate their school districts through often turbulent waters. Self-renewal today is a vitally important ingredient to staying energized and maintaining a clear perspective.

Covey refers to the process of self-renewal as "sharpening the saw." For him, the habit of sharpening the saw regularly means having a balanced, systematic program for self-renewal in four areas of our lives: physical, mental, emotional, and spiritual. He says that without discipline the body becomes weak, the mind mechanical, the emotions raw, the spirit insensitive, and the person selfish.

Key Thought

Do whatever it takes to stay
energized and focused.

CHAPTER 33

Rely on Human Goodness

If you've been on the job as a school administrator for any length of time, the following scenario should sound all too familiar.

7:00 a.m. You arrive at work and begin reading your leftover mail from the previous day. The second letter you read is from an irate parent about an incident that occurred a week ago in math class.

7:30 a.m. You meet with your food services director who surprises you by tendering her resignation.

8:00 a.m. You are called to your middle school to deal with a waterline break that is flooding the building's basement.

8:30 a.m. You travel to your school bus garage for a two-hour unfair labor practice hearing with a disgruntled bus driver.

10:30 a.m. You return to your office and meet with one of your school board members who is trying to micromanage the work of your curriculum director.

11:30 a.m. On your way out the door to eat lunch, your spouse calls to tell you that the dog is sick and needs to be taken to the veterinarian and you're the only one available to do it.

And it is not even noon yet.

While this chain of events may not occur every day, it is not an uncommon snapshot of what it is like to be an educational leader. Educational leaders spend much of their time dealing with problem situations and problematic people. Then, they return home only to turn on the television news and spend another 30 minutes or more being bombarded by stories of human suffering and tragedy.

As a result of the amount of time educational leaders are exposed to problems, it is easy for them to feel the effects of the negativity that surrounds them. Many become emotionally drained while some retreat to safe havens and disconnect from other people.

Unfortunately, when educational leaders insulate themselves from others, they lose perspective. This, in turn, leads to making mistakes in judgment.

However, there is a strategy for combating negativity. It is to awaken the goodness that exists in all of us.

In her book *Turning to One Another* (2002), Margaret Wheatley reminds us that although we live in a time of distress, numbness, and fear, people are still basically good and caring. She explains that we can trigger this goodness by turning to one another and discovering what we care about.

Real listening always brings us closer together. It validates us as human beings and, in the process, releases large reserves of human goodness that are lying just beneath the surface waiting to be tapped.

Key Thought

Rely on human goodness to help you
maintain a positive perspective
and use it to bring out the best in others.

CHAPTER 34

Believe the Honeymoon Doesn't Have to End

When a person begins a new job, the first few weeks or months are often referred to as the honeymoon period. The assumption is that since all good things must come to an end, the honeymoon also will end.

In effect, the honeymoon ends because we believe it will end. In Napoleon Hill's words, our fate becomes what we think about.

Just as the honeymoon in a new job ends because we believe it will end, the life of an educational leader sometimes turns south because we believe it will turn south. Our belief becomes a self-fulfilling prophecy.

But what if we not just believed but knew deep down that the honeymoon period of an educational leader does not have to end? What if educational leaders moved to this new paradigm of a never-ending honeymoon?

Prior to his retirement in 2003, Charlie Irish enjoyed an extended honeymoon for 13 years as superintendent of the Medina City Schools in Medina, Ohio. In his own words, this is how he did it:

> When I first became a superintendent, I enjoyed the community celebration about my appointment, but I knew that it would soon wane as I began to deal with some difficult issues. Fortunately, I had a trusted advisor who saw to it that I spent time talking with the staff and community in nontraditional ways. I visited people in their homes, I invited them into mine, and I randomly called citizens to join me in conversations about the schools.
>
> While the discussions migrated in a variety of directions and levels of depth, the most important role I played was that of listener. All that I heard seemed disjointed at first, but over time it came together as the community and I began to understand one another.

Most importantly, we developed a level of mutual trust and respect that got us through the inevitable hard times. Just as in a marriage, the honeymoon can continue indefinitely if the partners genuinely work to nurture their relationship.

Reaching the point of "knowing" that your honeymoon as an educational leader doesn't have to end will trigger your instincts to guide you to do what it takes to enjoy an extended honeymoon period.

Key Thought

Join the ranks of educational leaders
who have enjoyed extended honeymoons
throughout their careers.

CHAPTER 35

Summary of Key Thoughts

1. Empower good-hearted people to go out and make a difference.
2. Saving money in the short run may cost you more money in the long run.
3. Telling the whole truth builds trust and fosters understanding.
4. When you do things others should be doing, it wastes your time, limits what you are able to accomplish, and sets you up as a scapegoat for the mistakes of others.
5. When you allow nagging problems to fester, they infect your entire organization and ultimately your credibility.
6. Inspiring others with your heartfelt passion triggers a domino effect that works through your entire organization.
7. Embracing controversy can defuse problems and generate the will and wherewithal to solve them.
8. Most people need to be understood more than they need to be right.
9. Challenge the conventional wisdom that drives what others in your profession do.
10. Help people use their natural talents to help you succeed.
11. Hire people who are motivated by an inner drive to produce results and be a part of something great, and get rid of those who aren't.
12. The brutal facts generate real answers.
13. Make the change process work for you rather than against you.
14. Use transition periods as windows of opportunity to preserve the best of the past and secure the future.
15. What we don't understand we often don't support.

16. When you give others responsibility, they tend to act responsibly.
17. Work with everyone but spend the most time developing your best people.
18. Some solutions create more problems than they resolve.
19. We become what we think about both as individuals and as organizations.
20. Studying quantum theory will help you see problems in a different light and generate solutions that previously didn't exist.
21. Recognizing the patterns that shape behavior gives you the power (or leverage) to change them.
22. While feel-good strategies may work in the short run, they often generate negative, unintended consequences in the long run.
23. By selling problems rather than solutions, you can create the sense of urgency required to clarify needs and bring people together to work through issues and concerns to create positive change.
24. Tactics drive strategies as much as or more than strategies drive tactics.
25. Be careful what you say because more people than you think may be listening.
26. When the "choir" doesn't help drive important decisions, others will twist the intent of these decisions and turn them against you.
27. Building consensus through the power of the grapevine is a step-by-step process that can be shaped and controlled.
28. The energy generated by a crisis provides the impetus for change and renewal.
29. Rather than who you are or the position you hold, it is your ability to energize others that gives you the power to make a difference.
30. When making an important decision, the public needs to be given time to work through its impact and become comfortable with it.
31. Identify barriers that are getting in your way and create strategies to eliminate them.
32. Do whatever it takes to stay energized and focused.
33. Rely on human goodness to help you maintain a positive perspective and use it to bring out the best in others.
34. Join the ranks of educational leaders who have enjoyed extended honeymoons throughout their careers.

Bibliography
An Invitation to Continue Your Journey

As stated at the outset, this book is not about silver bullets and other quick fixes. Rather, it is a personal invitation for you to begin a journey into a new world of possibility which will enable you to extend your honeymoon period and safely navigate the rough waters of change.

Throughout, references have been made to visionaries who live or have lived on the leading edge of this new world. You are now invited to continue your journey by reading their works, which are listed below.

Bolman, Lee G. and Terrence E. Deal. *Leading with Soul: An Uncommon Journey of Spirit*. San Francisco: Jossey-Bass, 1995.

Buckingham, Marcus and Curt Coffman. *First, Break All the Rules: What the World's Greatest Managers Do Differently*. New York: Simon & Schuster, 1999.

Callahan, Raymond E. *Education and the Cult of Efficiency: A Study of the Social Forces That Have Shaped the Administration of the Public Schools*. Chicago and London: The University of Chicago Press, 1962.

Collins, Jim. *Good to Great: Why Some Companies Make the Leap . . . and Others Don't*. New York: HarperCollins, 2001.

Covey, Stephen R. *The Seven Habits of Highly Effective People*. New York: Summit Books, 1989.

Eastridge, Harry E. and William G. O'Callaghan, Jr. *When the Choir Began to Sing: A Story about Awakening the Leader within Each of Us*. Manhattan, KS: The MASTER Teacher, 2002.

Evans, Robert. *The Human Side of School Change: Reform, Resistance, and the Real-life Problems of Innovation.* San Francisco: Jossey-Bass, 1996.

Gladwell, Malcolm. *The Tipping Point: How Little Things Can Make a Big Difference*. Boston: Little, Brown and Company, 2000.

The Harwood Group. *Meaningful Chaos: How People Form Relationships with Public Concerns.* Dayton, OH: Kettering Foundation, 1993.

Hill, Napoleon. *Think and Grow Rich.* New York: Ballantine Books, 1937.

Hurst, David K. *Crisis & Renewal: Meeting the Challenge of Organizational Change.* Boston: Harvard Business School Press, 1995.

Kotter, John P. *Leading Change.* Boston: Harvard Business School Press, 1996.

O'Callaghan, William G., Jr. *The Power of Public Engagement: A Beacon of Hope for America's Schools.* Manhattan, KS: The MASTER Teacher, 1999.

Oncken, W. and D. Wass. "Management time: Who's got the monkey?" *Harvard Business Review*, Nov.–Dec. 1974; 75–80.

Senge, Peter M. *The Fifth Discipline: The Art and Practice of the Learning Organization.* New York: Doubleday, 1990.

Toffler, Alvin. *Powershift: Knowledge, Wealth, and Violence at the Edge of the 21st Century.* New York: Bantam, 1990.

Wheatley, Margaret J. *Leadership and the New Science: Learning about Organization from an Orderly Universe.* San Francisco: Berrett-Koehler, 1990.

———. *Turning to One Another: Simple Conversations to Restore Hope to the Future.* San Francisco: Berrett-Koehler, 2002.

Williamson, Marianne. *The Healing of America.* New York: Simon & Schuster, 1997.

Yankelovich, Daniel. *Coming to Public Judgment: Making Democracy Work in a Complex World.* New York: Syracuse University Press, 1991.

Index

About the Author

William G. O'Callaghan Jr. has spent a quarter of a century working with educational leaders. A former journalist, political consultant, and Fortune 500 corporate executive, he has developed a unique perspective about educational leadership, which he shares in this book.

He is the editor of *The Power of Public Engagement: A Beacon of Hope for America's Schools*, author of *Putting the Power of Public Engagement to Work for Your Schools and Community,* and coauthor of *When the Choir Began to Sing: A Story about Awakening the Leader within Each of Us*.